Written and compiled by Lois Rock
Illustrations copyright © 2010 Sophie Allsopp
This edition copyright © 2010 Lion Hudson

A Lion Children's Book
an imprint of
Lion Hudson plc
Wilkinson House, Jordan Hill Road,
Oxford OX2 8DR, England
www.lionhudson.com
ISBN 978 0 7459 6152 1

First edition 2010
This printing March 2010
1 3 5 7 9 10 8 6 4 2

Acknowledgments
All unattributed prayers are by Lois Rock, copyright © Lion Hudson.
The prayer by Sophie Piper is copyright © Lion Hudson.
Prayer by Mother Teresa (on page 15) used by permission.

Bible extracts are taken or adapted from the Good News Bible, published by
The Bible Societies/HarperCollins Publishers Ltd, UK
© American Bible Society 1966, 1971, 1976, 1992, used by permission.

The Bible extract on page 16 is taken from the Holy Bible, New International Version,
copyright © 1973, 1978, 1984 International Bible Society. Used by permission of Zondervan and Hodder
& Stoughton Limited. All rights reserved. The 'NIV' and 'New International Version' trademarks are
registered in the United States Patent and Trademark Office by International Bible Society. Use of either
trademark requires the permission of International Bible Society. UK trademark number 1448790.

The Lord's Prayer (on page 6) from *Common Worship: Services and Prayers for the Church of England*
(Church House Publishing, 2000) is copyright © The English Language Liturgical Consultation,
1988 and is reproduced by permission of the publishers.

A catalogue record for this book is available
from the British Library

Typeset in 17/20 Caslon Old Face BT
Printed and bound in China by Printplus Ltd

Distributed by:
UK: Marston Book Services Ltd, PO Box 269, Abingdon, Oxon OX14 4YN
USA: Trafalgar Square Publishing, 814 N Franklin Street, Chicago, IL 60610
USA Christian Market: Kregel Publications, PO Box 2607, Grand Rapids, MI 49501

Our FATHER

and other classic prayers for children

Lois Rock

Illustrated by Sophie Allsopp

LION
CHILDREN'S

The prayer that Jesus taught

Our Father in heaven,
hallowed be your name,
your kingdom come,
your will be done,
on earth as in heaven.
Give us today our daily bread.
Forgive us our sins
as we forgive those who sin against us.
Lead us not into temptation
but deliver us from evil.

The Our Father, or Lord's Prayer

For the kingdom, the power,
and the glory are yours
now and for ever.
Amen.

An ancient ending for the prayer

Morning prayers

O God,
I will pray to you in the morning,
I will pray to you at sunrise.

I will ask you to show me
the way that I should go.

I will trust in you to protect me,
I will trust in your love.

From Psalm 5

For this new morning and its light,
For rest and shelter of the night,
For health and food, for love and friends,
For every gift your goodness sends,
We thank you, gracious Lord.

Anonymous

9

Learning to pray

Here I am beneath the sky
and all alone in prayer;
but I know God is listening,
for God is everywhere.

O God,
It is so hard to keep my mind on my prayers.
My thoughts just run away in a butterfly
meadow of daydreams. Bring me back to the
path that will lead me into your presence.

Praise

All things bright and beautiful,
All creatures great and small,
All things wise and wonderful,
The Lord God made them all.

Cecil Frances Alexander (1818–95)

You alone, O God, deserve
praise and glory,
because of your constant love
and faithfulness.

Psalm 115:1

Let us with a gladsome mind
Praise the Lord for he is kind;
For his mercies shall endure,
Ever faithful, ever sure.

John Milton (1608–74)

Love

Love is giving, not taking,
mending, not breaking,
trusting, believing,
never deceiving,
patiently bearing
and faithfully sharing
each joy, every sorrow,
today and tomorrow.

Anonymous

We can do no great things,
Only small things with great love.

Mother Teresa of Calcutta (1910–97)

Forgiveness

From the mud, a pure white flower,
From the storm, a clear blue sky.
As we pardon one another
God forgives us from on high.

Sophie Piper

God, have mercy on me, a sinner.

The Jesus Prayer, from Luke 18:13

I told God everything:
I told God about all the wrong things I had done.
I gave up trying to pretend.
I gave up trying to hide.
I knew that the only thing to do was to confess.

And God forgave me.

Based on Psalm 32:5

Thanks

The harvest of our garden
is astonishingly small;
but oh, dear God, we thank you
that there's anything at all.

For health and strength
and daily food,
we praise your name,
O Lord.

Traditional

18

I give thanks for the people
who are my home:
we share a place to shelter;
we share our food;
we share our times of work
and play and rest;
we share our lives.

God is great, God is good,
Let us thank him for our food.

Traditional

19

Journeys

Father, lead us through this day
As we travel on our way.
Be our safety, be our friend,
Bring us to our journey's end.

20

May the road rise to meet you.
May the wind be always at your back.
May the sun shine warm upon your face,
the rains fall soft upon your fields and,
until we meet again,
may God hold you in the palm of his hand.

Irish blessing

Sadness

Lord, make me an instrument of your peace.
Where there is hatred, let me sow love;
Where there is injury, pardon;
Where there is discord, union;
Where there is doubt, faith;
Where there is despair, hope;
Where there is darkness, light;
Where there is sadness, joy.

A prayer traditionally attributed to St Francis of Assisi (1181–1226)

Deeply gloomy
Deeply sad
When the day
Goes deeply bad.

Deeply hoping
God above
Will enfold me
In his love.

Comfort

The Lord is my shepherd;
  I have everything I need.
He lets me rest in fields of green grass
  and leads me to quiet pools of fresh water.
He gives me new strength.
He guides me in the right paths,
  as he has promised.
Even if I go through the deepest darkness,
  I will not be afraid, Lord,
  for you are with me.
Your shepherd's rod and staff protect me.

Psalm 23:1–5

O God,
be to me
like the evergreen tree
and shelter me in your shade,
and bless me again
like the warm gentle rain
that gives life to all you have made.

Based on Hosea 14:4–8

Blessings

Deep peace of the running waves to you,
Deep peace of the flowing air to you,
Deep peace of the quiet earth to you,
Deep peace of the shining stars to you,
Deep peace of the shades of night to you,
Moon and stars always giving light to you,
Deep peace of Christ, the Son of Peace, to you.

Traditional Gaelic blessing

May God bless you and take care of you.
May God be kind to you and do good things for you.
May God look on you with love and give you peace.

From Numbers 6

May the grace of the Lord Jesus be with everyone.

Revelation 22:21, the last line of the Bible

Night

The sunrise
tells of God's glory;
the moonrise
tells of God's glory;
the starshine
tells of God's glory;
the heavens
tell of God's glory.

Based on Psalm 19

When I lie down, I go to sleep
    in peace;
you alone, O Lord, keep me
    perfectly safe.

Psalm 4:8

Now I lay me down to sleep,
I pray thee, Lord, thy child to keep;
Thy love to guard me through the night
And wake me in the morning light.

Traditional

Index of first lines